Jacob,

Grandpa Salts gave this cookbook to Uncle Dave so he could cook for Aunt Nell.

I thought that Uncle Dave would like it if you & Daddy cooked for Mommy & Sarah.

Wolf in CHEF'S Clothing

The pictures make cooking easy & FUN!!

I hope you & your family enjoy cooking "Wolf-style".

LOVE

Aunt Nell

Wolf

in CHEF'S Clothing

by Robert H. Loeb, Jr.
illustrated by Jim Newhall

THE **picture** COOK AND DRINK BOOK FOR MEN

SURREY BOOKS Chicago

WOLF IN CHEF'S CLOTHING

4th edition
is published by Surrey Books, Inc.
230 E. Ohio St., Suite 120, Chicago, IL 60611

5 4 3 2 1

Printed and bound in Hong Kong by C&C Offset Printing Co., Ltd.

Library of Congress Cataloging-in-Publication Data
Loeb, Robert H.
Wolf in chef's clothing : the picture cook and drink book for men / by Robert H. Loeb, Jr. ;
illustrated by Jim Newhall.—4th ed.
p. cm.
Originally published: The new wolf in chef's clothing. c1958.
Includes index.
ISBN 1-57284-035-8 (paper)
1. Cookery. I. Loeb, Robert H. New wolf in chef's clothing. II. Title
TX652 .L4218 2000
641.5—dc21

A note about the book and the creative team

WOLF IN CHEF'S CLOTHING was originally published in Chicago in 1950. At that time, the city was a broadcasting and advertising mecca; agency giants Leo Burnett and Foote Cone & Belding were headquartered there. *Esquire* magazine had been going strong since the 1930s, and "The Breakfast Club," "Kukla, Fran and Ollie," "Quiz Kids," and other network TV and radio programs emanated from Chicago studios.

ROBERT H. LOEB, JR., the author, was food and drink editor for *Esquire* magazine in the early 1950s. When the magazine moved from Chicago to New York, Bob went with it, and continued to write hundreds of magazine articles and more than ten books. Illustrator JIM NEWHALL was art director for a large Chicago advertising agency and promotion director for two Chicago newspapers.

table of contents

dedication

To my father, and my father's father, and my father's father's father, right back to Adam, all of whom spent their lives as the passive victims of feminine culinary caprice–from that first apple to apfelstrudel.

And to the little woman, too, and the middle-sized woman, and the big woman–in fact, all women; the connubial-bliss type and the convivial-miss type, all of whom have been tangled for centuries in the maze of cookbook hieroglyphics, cuneiform and Sanskrit.

measuring symbols

That's all—nothing more to it. *No teaspoons at all,* no fractional "ozzes," converting litres to quarts—no special measuring instruments of any kind. If you're worried about exactly how much a tablespoon is, forget it. Just use an ordinary one, and fill it up above level. The same applies for a cup. And for half of either, just be approximate. The art of cooking, like the art of love-making, depends more on the proper use of ingredients than on their exact quantitative measurements. So relax, wolf, when you mix, and bark joyously when you stir. Never be tense and growl; remember in order to make that dish you're supposed to be placid like the sheep—a veritable lamb. Get what I mean, old chop?

PART I

cooking with pictures

THERE probably have been as many cookbooks written as there are recipes. Tomes printed in fine type for wives, matrons, chefs, gourmets—about what Martha Washington served, Mom's favorite dishes, the "Selected Recipes of the Confederated Clubs of All-Women Members of Apidula, North Carolina," etc., etc.

No one really ever considered the male animal who didn't want to know how to cook carp according to a rare Tibetan recipe, or pore through a hundred lines of instructions so that he could turn out the dessert that Madame de Pompadour served Louis XV on September 18, 1748. In fact, no one ever considered that man, a man (except, of course, Louis), is just as anxious, and under just as much obligation, to be a good host as woman is to be a hostess. He's equally as desirous of knowing how to prepare simple, pleasing dishes—or drinks—for friend or "femme."

The purpose of this book is to enfranchise the male, to unshackle him from the role of refrigerator vulture, icebox scavenger, from being a parasitic gourmet forced to feed on the leftovers of female cookery. Instead, he can become a gustatory eagle, king of the kitchen, and baron of the bar.

And where does he go from there? He can shine as a host by being able to serve custom-made snacks and drinks, not factory-made ones. He'll no longer be a slave to the maître d'hôtel—he'll be his own. And think of the money he'll save. And if he's a married man, consider the scope this new art can give him. For state occasions, anniversaries, birthdays, Mother's Days, guilt and appeasement days, he won't just be limited to flowers and mink. He'll be able to serve a brunch, a supper, or a breakfast fit for a queen—and let her do the dishes for a change. It's a saving all around. In fact, he'll be able to make a simple dish for every occasion—midday, midnight, maid's night off, and for some special persuasion.

And how is this magical transformation of the male animal accomplished? The instructions in the average cookbook are as terrifying as those on an income-tax form. While you're wrestling with some fragile eggs in one hand, you're to refer back to Paragraph C, Section 39 (you have to turn back three pages with the other hand to do that, too) and, at the same time, you are to measure out three milligrams of baking powder with some astral third hand, constantly stirring the sauce that's supposed to be simmering—but seems to be singeing—with yet a fourth hand. That's all right for an octopus, but who wants to be an octopus? A squid. But that sort of multimanual activity is not for man.

Instead, all impractical recipes have been sifted out; only those that are of immediate use—simple, tasty, and pleasingly garnished—have been included. The recipes are presented with pictures—wringing out all verbiage—and I mean *all*. The modern, unshackled man can throw out all measurements such as grams, "ozzes" (ounces), milligrams, quarts, litres, and apothecary scales. While you're cooking or mixing even a complicated dish or drink, you don't have to read through line after line of fine type to find out what your next step is. It's all right there in picture form, step by step. You can see at a glance from conception to perfection what the dish is going to be.

And what's more, all recipes are catalogued for the occasion. You don't have to pore through page after page of occult reading matter to figure out what to serve. If you want to make breakfast, turn to the breakfast section. For lunch, supper, midnight snacks, ditto. And drinks—it's a tickler deciding when to serve what. WOLF IN CHEF'S CLOTHING takes over the whole problem by putting drinks in their proper place: drinks for before meals, after meals, in-between meals, and with meals. See what I mean? You don't have to think. All you have to do is make like the pictures.

In fact, all that has been done is to codify the laws of cookery and drinkery in a manner long ago employed by the male animal—then called cave man. He was immortalized because he painted pictures on the walls of his habitat. Here is a return to that technique. Food and drink have been put into cave-man form—with pictures—and thus will open up a vast new realm of social opportunity for bewildered, modern man.

And woman, too.

PART II

breakfast for two

If you want to rise and shine —
    Make her breakfast.
If your conscience is bad —
    Make her breakfast.
If *her* conscience is bad —
    Make her breakfast.
If you want to breakfast her —
    Read on

A male in pajamas is a mussed, woolly, and amorphous thing. Even the best man looks no Don Juan at dawn — just wan. But there's a cure.

coffee – home-brew

drip – looks like this →

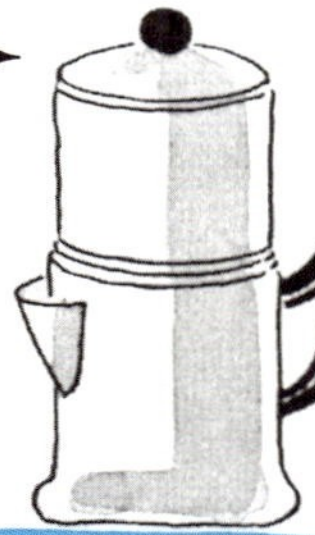

ingredients:

procedure:

1. boil

2. put in

3. pour

4. ready when dripped through

percolate — looks like this

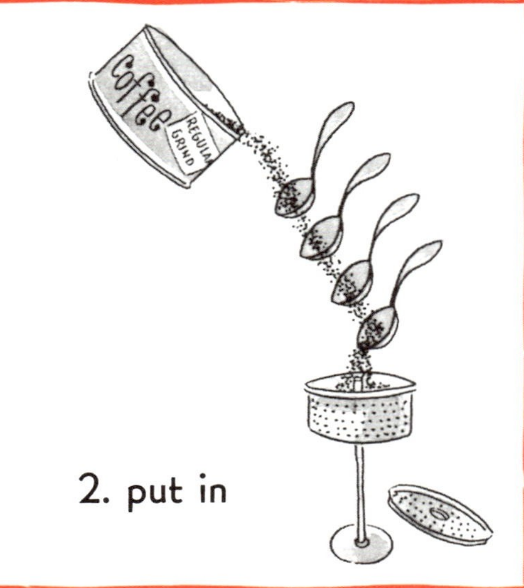

4. perc

5 min.

or **vaculate** — looks like this

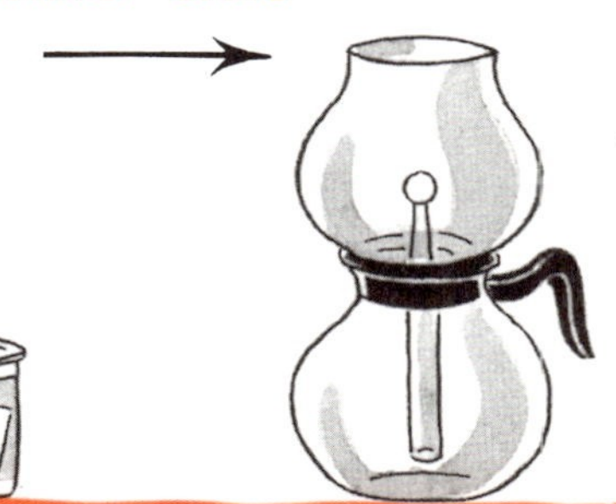

ingredients:

procedure:

1. pour

2. put in

3. assemble tightly

4. heat—
when H_2O
rises to
top,

turn off flame—when liquid returns to bottom—drink it—it's coffee!

grapefruit

ingredients:

procedure:

1. slice in two

2. cut around segments and trim

3. chill and garnish

strawberries

ingredients:

procedure:

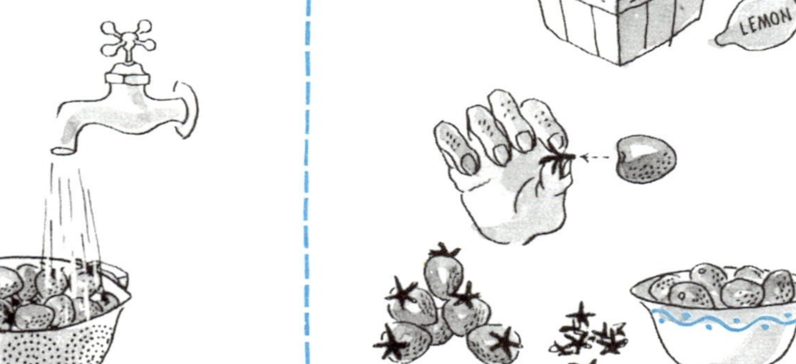

1. wash and pick out bad ones

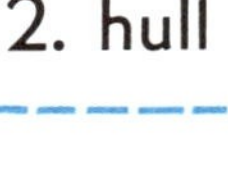

2. hull

3. sprinkle

4. add and mix

citrous fantasies
or how to juggle an orange

orange Hawaiian

ingredients:

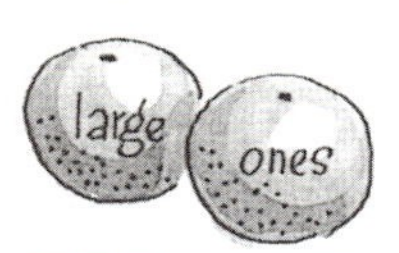

procedure:

1. cut—de-pulp—save shells

2. add to pulp

3. cook till looks like thin marmalade

4. heat's off—mix in

5. fill shells and sprinkle

6. bake—then let cool (not in refrigerator)

don't lay an **egg**

scramble, poach, fry
or hide it in an omele

scrambled

ingredients:

procedure:

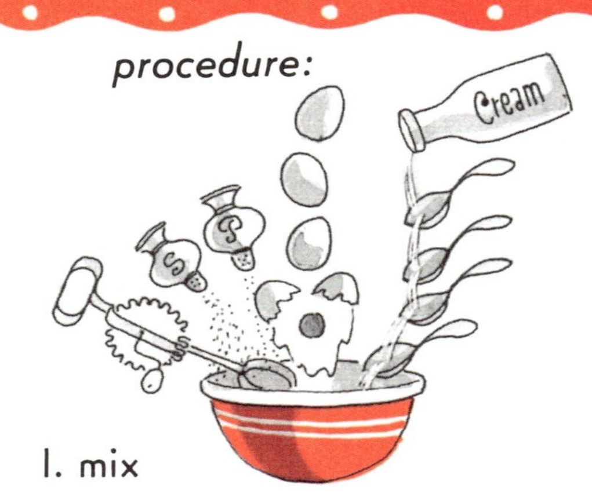

1. mix

2. melt and brown

3. pour and cook—low flame

4. stir until cooked through—serve

Easter scrambled

ingredients:

procedure:

1. mix

2. add and mix

3. melt and brown

4. pour and stir until done

shirred eggs

fried eggs

ingredients:

procedure:

1. melt until brown

2. add without breaking yolks!—slow fire

3. off fire when whites are firm—serve (repeat these steps for second batch)

eggs demi-benedict

ingredients:

5. while waiting for H_2O to boil, mix

6. add yolk only and mix

7. stir—heat very slowly until warm—your sauce is done

8. now to poach—

add to boiling water without breaking yolks—low flame

9. when whites solid, transfer gently

10. pour over each—and *voila!*

international **omelet** set

French

ingredients:

procedure:

1. mix and beat together

2. melt

3. pour—flame low

4. when solid, flip over—cook one minute—sprinkle

5. remove—roll up—serve *comme ça*

Spanish
ingredients:
Cream
BUTTER
PARSLEY
S
P
GREEN PEPPER
Tomatoes
OLIVE OIL
stuffed olives
procedure:
OLIVE OIL
1. heat
2. chop—
add—
cook
5 MIN.

Tomatoes
Stuffed olives
3. add—
cook
until it
thickens

french
4. make French omelet as on
preceding page—hurry!

french
5. pour
one-half
and roll

6. pour
on
balance—
serve *con mucho gusto*

ingredients:

BUTTER

1. separate whites and yolks

2. beat until stiff

3. add—beat

4. blend together—don't beat

5. melt

6. pour—flame low

7. when firm—remove—
place under broiler

8. when top is pale tan,
remove—sprinkle

9. put—roll—serve

le toast de Paris

don't try this unless you have a:

waffles

ingredients:

procedure:

1. separate and beat each

2. mix

3. melt

4. combine by beating

5. mix in gently—don't beat

6. pour on heated iron; remove when crisp tan—serve

her majesty's breakfast service

how to make a queen eat out of your hand next time, and save dishes

proper table setting

proper tray setting

sup — her

Here are four $10 specials graded for type:

menu #1

If she's the athletic type—long, lean, and limbsome, who prefers a game of tennis to a shot of 3-star Henness(ey):

tomato juice à l'ocean—mignon et béarnaise—baked potatoes—salad Roquefort

menu #2

If she's the indoor type—soft, round, and fluffy, who thinks Alexander the Great the best cocktail ever made:

broiled grapefruit—lamb chops—potatoes fried à la France—salade Walt Whitman

menu #3

If she's the intellectual type—more an I.Q. than a Q.T.—if she prefers Gounod's *Faust* to getting soused:

orange Hawaiian—spaghetti da Vinci—les choux froids

menu #4

If she's the 3-B type—brains, bonds, and beauty—don't believe it—but it's fun pretending:

strawberry loving cup—poulet maison dixon—potatoes à l'onion—salad subversive

tomato juice à l'océan

ingredients:

procedure:

1. mix

2. add and mix

3. pour and garnish

strawberry loving cup

ingredients:

procedure: 1. make with the orange juice and strawberries (page 16)

2. combine and stir

3. chill well

4. put in

5. add

broiled grapefruit

ingredients:

procedure:

1. prepare grapefruit

2. sprinkle

3. put under broiler

4. remove—garnish—serve

sea food Dorothea
serves four
ingredients:
FROZEN LOBSTER 8 oz.
FROZEN CRAB MEAT 8 oz.
MAYON-NAISE
SOUR CREAM
HORSE-RADISH
Chili Sauce
WOR-CESTER-SHIRE SAUCE
Lettuce
Hard Boiled
Lemon
Garlic
Kosher Dill Pickle
procedure:
FROZEN LOBSTER
FROZEN CRAB MEAT
1. defrost—
separate
pieces—
sprinkle
Sour Cream
Chili Sauce
Mayon-naise
2. mix in
separate bowl
HORSE-RADISH
3. add
WORCESTER-SHIRE SAUCE
4. and
5. arrange each portion so
6. pour over each—serve

wolf-fare — the carnivore's baedecker

steak – noble (sir-loin) or t-beian (t-bone)

and meanwhile—
6 MIN.
each side
for rare
4. give gas full throttle—place
as close to broiler flame as
possible—leave door
open two inches
5. remove like so
6. mix together—
heat one minute
7. pour over—serve

mignon et béarnaise a carnivore's opera

5. add—and keep stir-ring! when smooth, the sauce is done

6. now the fillet—wrap around and secure like this—add

7. melt and heat well

8. add

9. now place in broiler

10. remove—pour over—serve

lamb chops the amazing meat that goes in like a lamb and comes out like a chop

poulet maison dixon

un-American activities gastronomic recipe serves four

spaghetti da Vinci

ingredients:

procedure:

1. heat

2. chop—fry till tan

3. add—mix in

4. add—cook till meat is done

5. remove and transfer

6. add—stir in

7. add—stir in

8. cover—cook slowly

9. put in boiling water

10. remove when soft and drain

11. transfer

12. remove sauce—mix in

13. pour over—sprinkle

14. serve along with

shrimps cobra

ingredients:

procedure:

1. add to six cups boiling water—cook

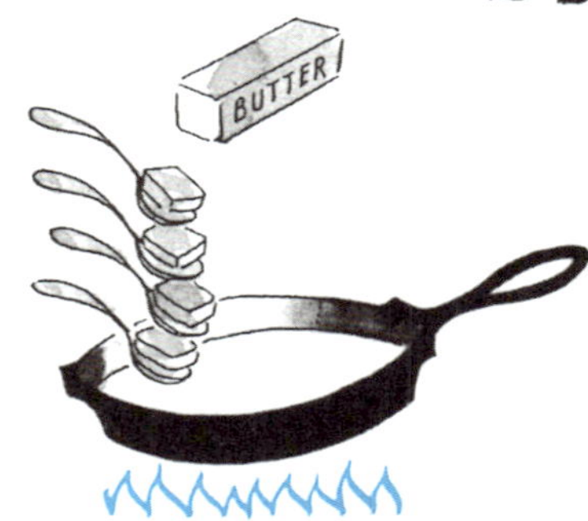

2. meanwhile—melt

3. chop—fry till tender

4. add

5. pour juice only—add

6. pour into

7. add

8. add

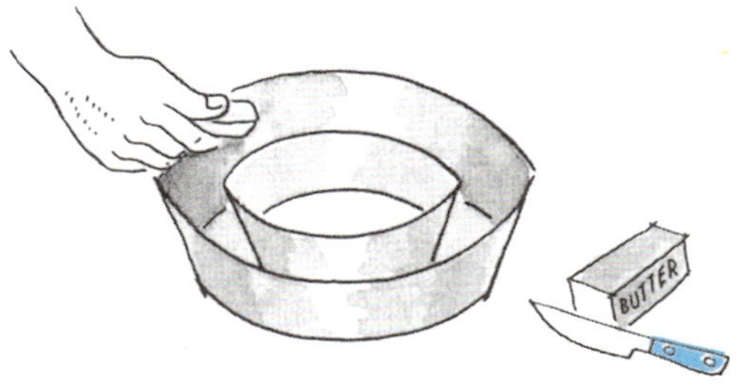

9. add—cook slowly

10. now—grease mold well

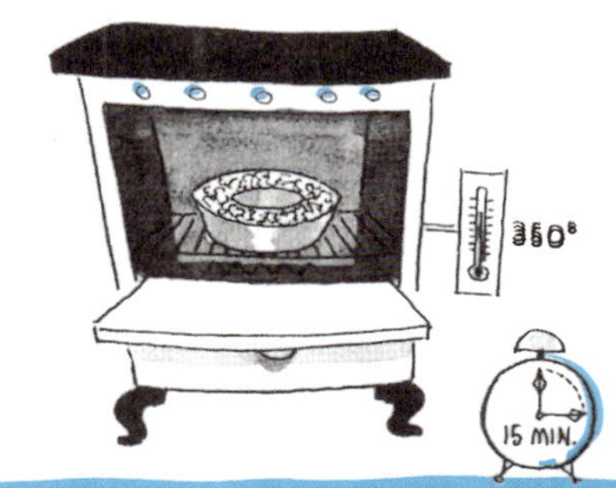

11. transfer rice—pack in well

12. bake

13. unmold—pour in center

14. serve with

hamburgers sans ham
ingredients:
Chopped Round Steak
1½ LBS.
GREEN PEPPER
Rye Bread
BUTTER
S
P
procedure:
1. knead together
2. chop and add
3. add and knead well
4. make into four fat disks
5. melt until brown
6. fry each side according to desired rareness
7. serve

potatoes here's spuds in your eye

baked

ingredients:

procedure:

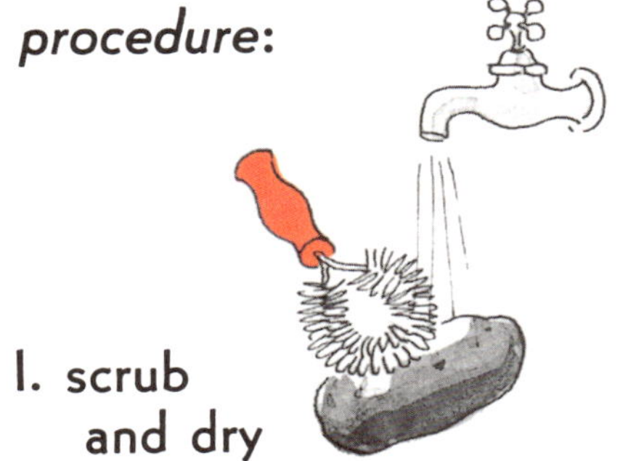

1. scrub and dry

2. rub all over

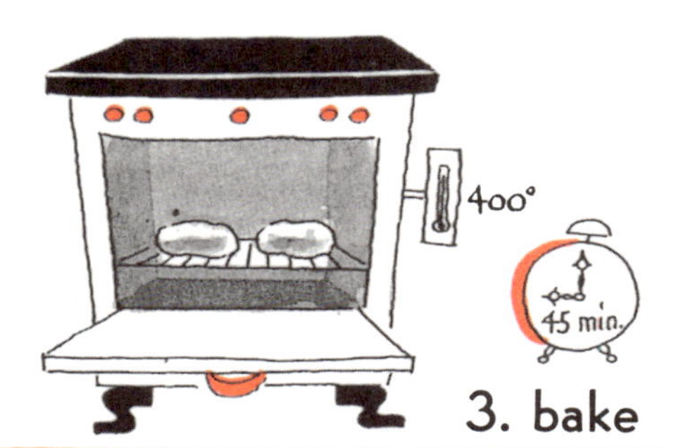

3. bake

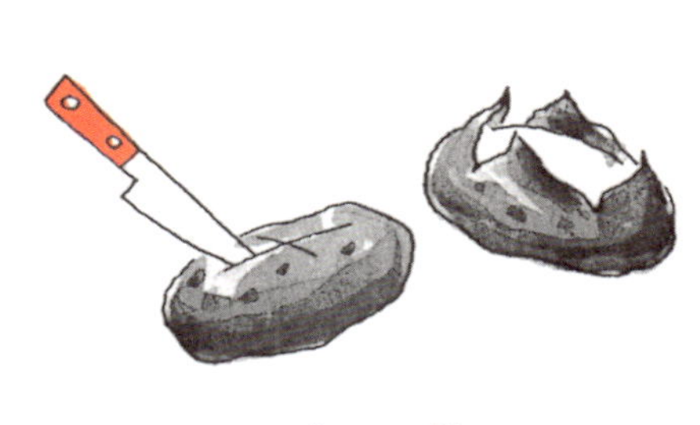

4. split

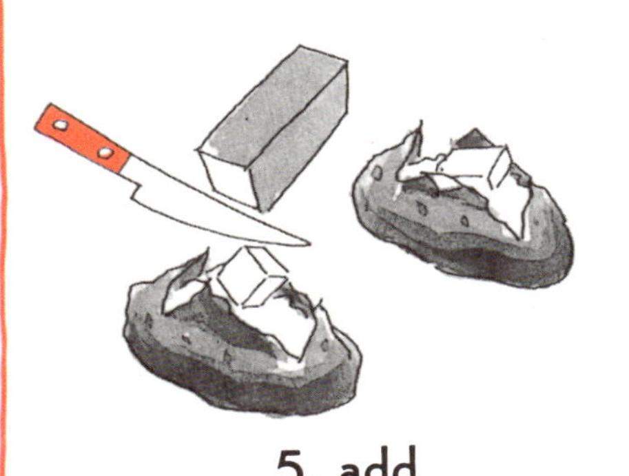

5. add

6. sprinkle and serve

potatoes à l'onion

fried à la France

salads containing the new, amazing medical discovery: chlorophyll

serves four

salade Walt Whitman

salade Roquefort serves four

ingredients:

(see page 55)

procedure:

1. cut into chunks—use the entire head

2. break up and add

3. add—toss well—serve

asparagus salad

ingredients:

procedure:

1. beat till thick

2. add and mix in

3. arrange on lettuce bed

4. pour over—serve

salade subversive

ingredients:

(see page 56)

procedure:

1. cut two wedges

2. cut into quarters

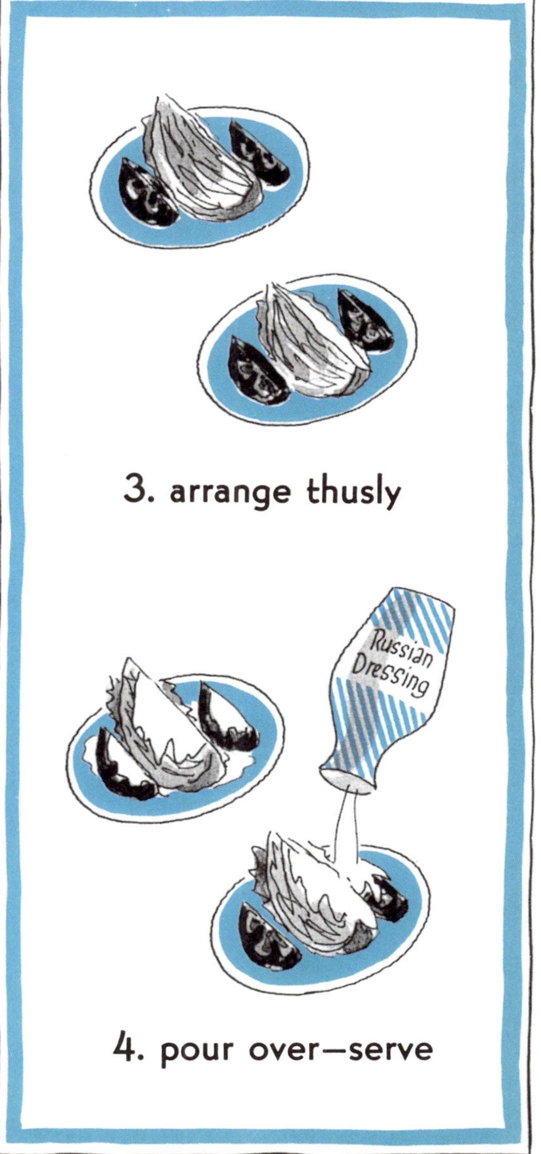

3. arrange thusly

4. pour over—serve

les choux froids cole slaw to you

ingredients:

procedure:

1. mix

2. add and mix

3. and

4. shred—use whole head

5. pour over—toss well

6. garnish and serve

salad dressing room

ingredients:

Russian dressing

ingredients:

procedure:

1. mix

2. and

3. and

4. mix well—serve

PART IV

midsupper's night dream

ALONG toward midnight, when conversation is limping and tongues idly flopping, and the heat's off, and the fire's burned out, and your guests are drooping over their chairs like Dali's limp clocks—there's a way to resurrect rather than bury them.

Creep off to your kitchenette; whip up one of these suggested dishes. Lusterless eyes will sparkle again, tongues clack with vivacity, and sufficient energy will have been imbued in your guests to enable them to eventually put on their coats and depart with a pleasant after-image in their minds—and tummies.

Welsh rabbit serves four

1. trim

2. keep warm

3. start melting slowly—do not allow to boil

4. add

5. cheese almost melted—add

6. stir until absorbed

7. remove—pour over—
sprinkle—serve

salmon salad Marguerite

for a hot night

1. mix

2. chop and add

3. add

4. and mix in

5. garnish and serve

hot snack Marie

serves four

ingredients:

procedure:

1. defrost—separate pieces

2. toast—one side only

3. place—toasted side down

4. slice into four pieces—place

5. add

6. broil till cheese is melted

follies minuit
serves 4
ingredients:
S
P
BUTTER
FLOUR
XXX
tomatoes
SUGAR
MILK
BACON
procedure:
1. boil
10 min.
2. meanwhile melt
FLOUR
XXX
3. add and stir
MILK
S
P
4. add and stir until thick
5. add
FLOUR
XXX
S
SUGAR
6. mix separately

7. dip both sides
8. fry till crisp
9. fry in bacon fat
until crusty
10. toast
11. combine
12. pour over—serve

spareribs barbecue

ingredients:

procedure:

1. cut into two rib sections—broil until brown—remove

2. heat

3. slice fine—fry till tan

4. add

5. and

6. and—simmer

7. pour over one-half

8. bake

baste with balance of sauce while baking

crêpes suzettes

or—chafing just a bit (if you lack a chafing dish, substitute a deep frying pan)   serves four

ingredients:

procedure:

1. beat together

2. add, sifted, and beat

3. add, grated

4. add, melted, and beat in

OLIVE OIL
5. meanwhile heat
6. each crêpe 3″ in diameter
7. repeat hot oil, etc. for each batch—a total of twelve
1/4 LB.
8. crêpes done—put aside—melt in chafing dish
9. add, grated
SUGAR
10. and

Vanilla
11. and
12. put in—
cook till
sauce is
very syrupy
Powdered
Sugar
13. then
roll and
sprinkle
Cognac
Cointreau
14. add
15. ignite
16. gloat
and serve
three per

PART FIVE

prometheus
and charcoal gray

WHEN Prometheus stole the secret of fire from the gods and gave it to man, it is very doubtful that he realized the extent of harm he was doing. Aside from incipient incendiaries and hotfoot pranksters, he imbued a lot of men with the delusion that all you had to do to cook anything outdoors was simply to bring food in contact with the fire. The result of this has led to innumerable gastronomic and intestinal calamities, mainly due to charcoal-broiled steaks—where all that remains is the charcoal and no steak. The same thing happens with chops—and chicken often ends up as seared bones.

However, with proper instructions and a few basic, simple-to-follow recipes, the successful indoor wolf can become equally successful in the patio—provided there are enough cushions.

outdoor wolfing gear:

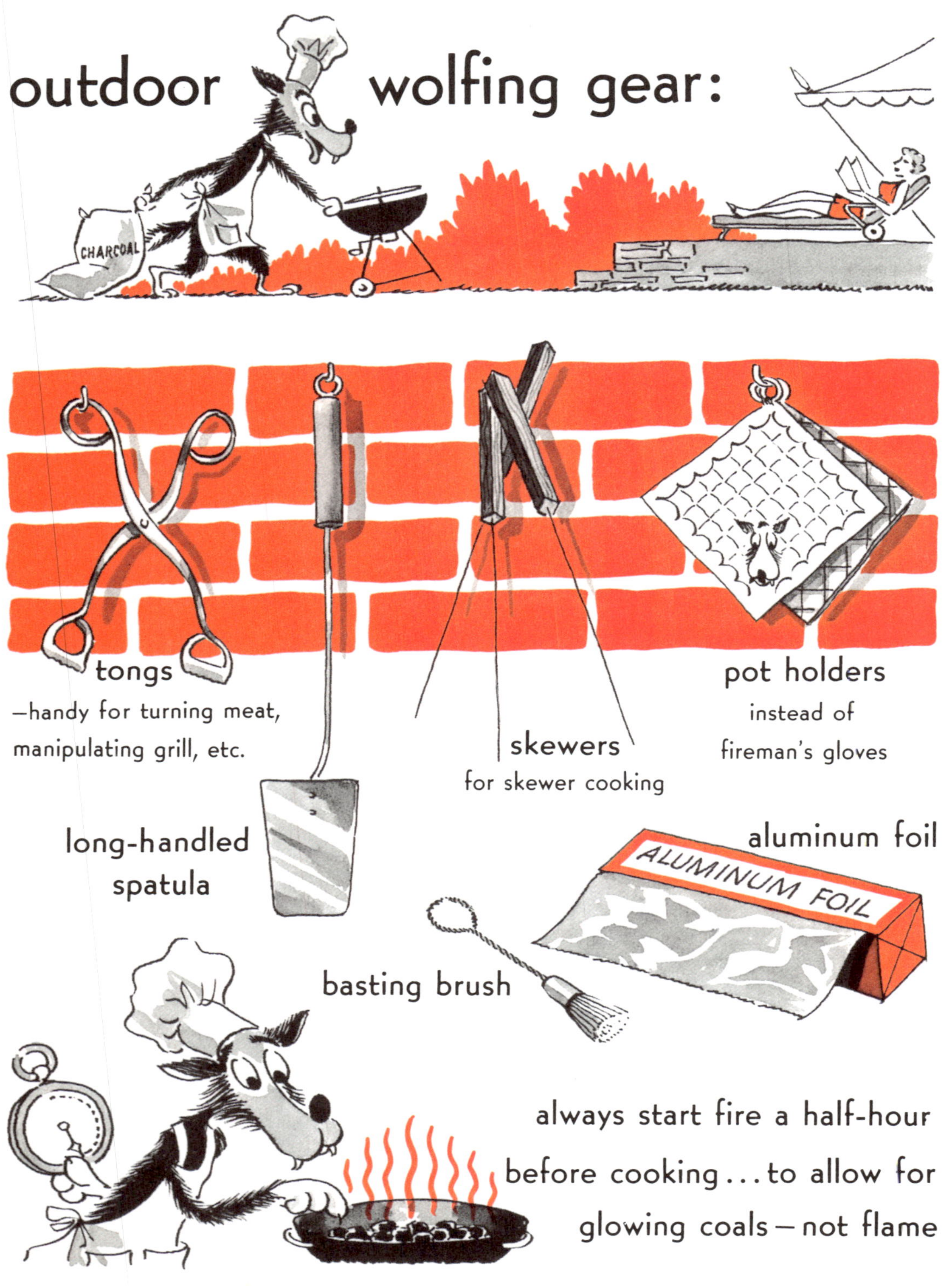

carnival for carnivores

meat cookery:

steaks — chops — wieners — spareribs — chicken

steakmanship broiling CHART:

	RARE	MEDIUM	WELL DONE
1 INCH THICK	5 MIN.	6 MIN.	8 MIN.
1½ INCHES THICK	9 MIN.	10 MIN.	13 MIN.
2 INCHES THICK	15 MIN.	17 MIN.	20 MIN.

steak Dinah – serves 6

ingredients:

tools:

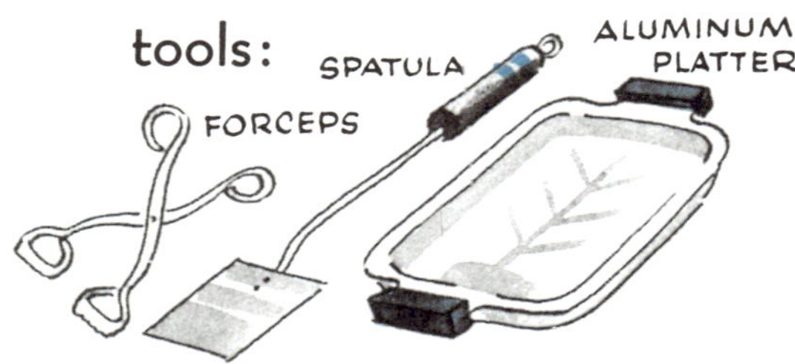

procedure:

1\.

smear all over steak, like oiling baby (both sides)

2\.

place on grill 3 inches above flame. follow fire directions on page 70

3\.

turn over – consult chart for timing. important! if flames get high, calm them down by sprinkling fire with water

4\.

when done, transfer to platter – then place platter on grill to put on sauce

and the **sauce**

ingredients:

tools:

procedure:

1\.

while steak is cooking, put in butter and cheese—

2\.

mush together thoroughly.

3\.

add and mix in thoroughly cut up—so—and mix in

the moment the steak's in the platter, add.

4\.

let sizzle a minute—serve!

cop-chops – serves 4

dinner wieners – serves 4

procedure:

1. slice ends – so

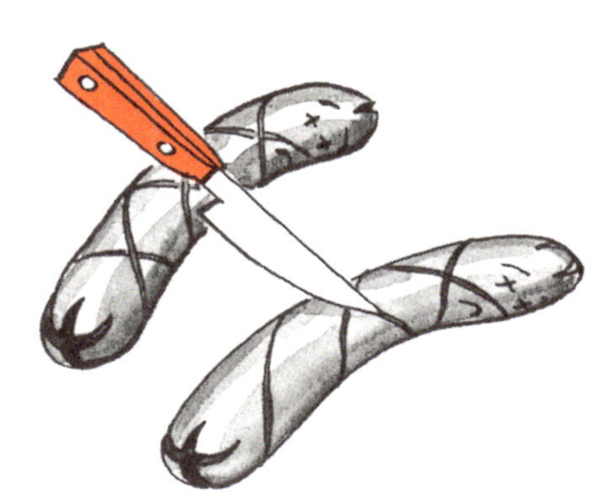

2. score sides crisscross – so

3. place on grill raised 3" above coals

4. roll over so all sides get cooked – when crisp around scored edges, serve with toasted wiener rolls

4-alarm chicken – serves 4

1. wash well – so – pat dry

2. place each half on a large piece of aluminum foil

3. apply oil on both sides – so

4. sprinkle with salt & pepper – add thyme and rosemary to each side

5. now apply chili sauce lightly to both sides

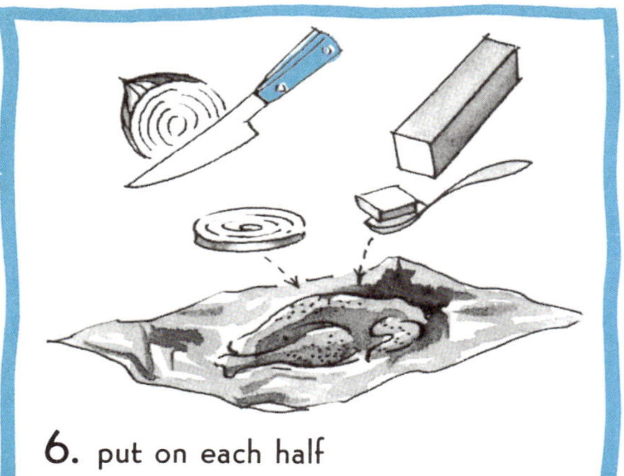

6. put on each half

wrap each carefully — then wrap in additional sheet of foil — place on grill raised 3 inches above flame.

8.

turn on other side after 15 minutes — cook 15 minutes more

9.

remove from fire & unwrap, pouring juice into platter.

10.

replace undressed chicken on grill — brown both sides about 2 min. each

11.

now place on platter — let juice boil 2 minutes — serve!

shrimpatizer – serves 4

ingredients:

tools:

SKEWERS

PARING KNIFE

procedure:

1. cut into wedges

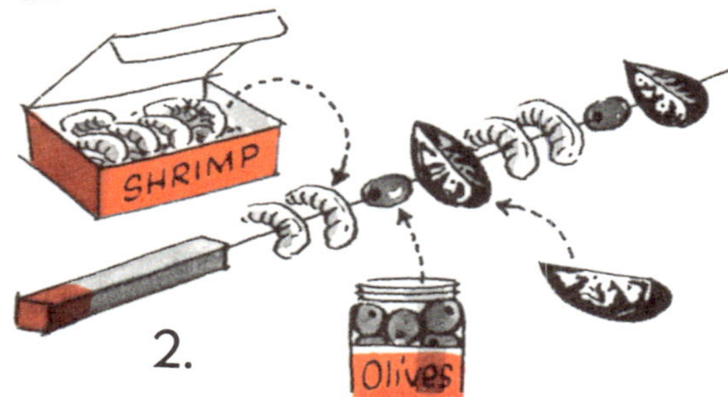

2. thread "spear" alternately with 2 shrimps, olive, and tomato

3. grill till shrimp's golden-tanned – turn frequently

wolfke bob
— serves 4
ingredients:
ROUND STEAK (2" CHUNKS)
2 LBS.
MUSHROOMS
1 LB.
RED TABLE WINE
Olive Oil
MEDIUM SIZED ONIONS
2 CLOVES GARLIC
PICKLING SPICE
OREGANO
S
P
tools:
SKEWERS
PARING KNIFE
procedure:
Olive Oil
RED TABLE WINE
THE NIGHT BEFORE
TEASPOONS
PICKLING SPICE
TABLESPOON
1. mix
2. and add...

3\.

again add —
and let stand overnight

4\.

wash — peel — cut off stems

5\. peel — slice onions in half

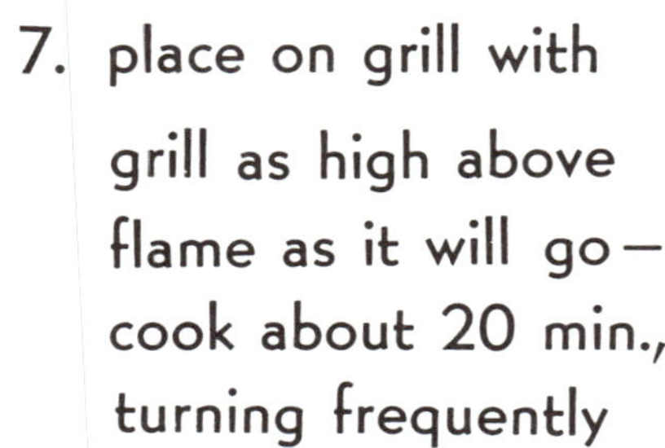

6\. spear in succession close together

7\. place on grill with grill as high above flame as it will go — cook about 20 min., turning frequently

lamb steak figaro–

serves 4

ingredients:

procedure:

1. combine in large bowl

2. and add…

3. coat each side with olive oil

4. sprinkle with salt and pepper

5. put on grill 3 inches above coals

6. baste with spoon constantly –

7. turn on other side after 10 min. and broil – baste constantly for 10 min.

8. transfer to platter – add remaining juice – sizzle few minutes – serve!

bread Français

ingredients:

procedure:

1. cut deep slit
2. slice three-fourths deep
3. melt
4. chop and stir in
5. pour into center trench
6. toast—serve hot

sitting duck Vincent – serves 4

ingredients:

tools:

procedure:

1. place each half on large sheet of foil, hollow sides up

2. mix in bowl

3. add

4. and add – stir

5.
transfer to saucepan – bring to boil,
stirring constantly
6.
fill cavities of duck
with ½ cup of sauce each
7.
carefully wrap and seal completely
30 MIN.
8. on grill – 30 min.
9.
unwrap –
pour juice into sauce pan with the sauce
10.
brown ducks on grill –
basting constantly
COGNAC
11.
when crisp,
tan each side – place on platter – cover
with sauce – sizzle – pour cognac over ducks
12.
drop lighted match into
platter – serve flaming hot

the hot banana

ingredients:

procedure:

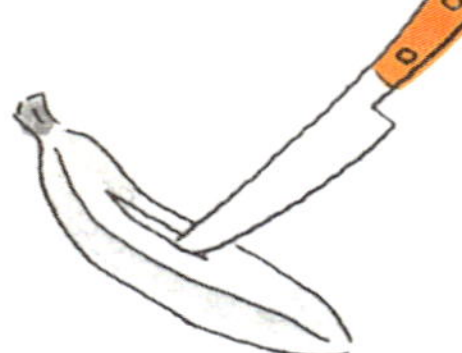

1. (do not peel)—make three-inch slit in skin

2. put in slit

3. place—turn each side cook 8 min. serve

barbecued tomatoes

ingredients:

procedure: (night before)

1. mix—let soak overnight

2. cut in half—baste

3. grill and baste—serve

PART VI

the solid teaser

—the cocktail canapé

THIS interesting gastronomic teaser is a paradox in every way. It does not whet one's appetite — but, instead, serves to whet one's thirst. The more you eat, the more you drink, which, combined, decreases your gustatory needs. *Quel* paradox!

This predicament has several advantages for the host: when serving cocktails before dinner, it will tend to cut down on unexpected inroads on your main repast. And canapés at cocktailtime tend to keep your guests on an even keel (albeit at the expense of your liquor supply).

Anyway, there is the canapé and as a host you've got to do better than just serving toast, or peanuts, or popcorn to lend éclat to your efforts.

So here's to the canapé — the cocktail snack — the midget meal — the salivary titillator — the drink-whetter and appetite-forgetter.

c'est la vie canapé

ingredients:

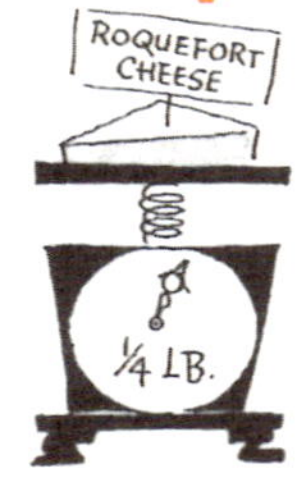

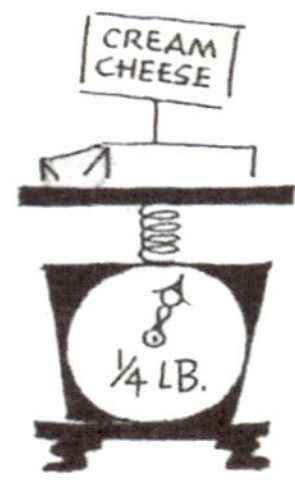

procedure:

1. mash

2. add and make paste

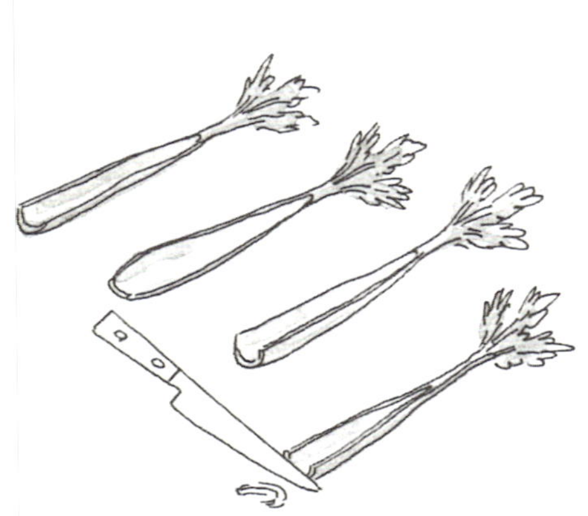

3. cut and separate stalks

4. fill each stalk

canapé fromage and strictly from hunger

ingredients:

Cream

Cream Cheese ½ LB.

ANCHOVY PASTE

PAPRIKA

WHITE BREAD

S

procedure:

fruit glass

1. cut out like so and toast

2. mix into paste

3. add and mix in

4. add finely chopped

5. spread—sprinkle for color

6. serve

urgéd sturgeon canapé

ingredients:

procedure:

1. hard boil and cool
2. then chop very fine
3. mix separately
4. add and mix
5. cut out and toast
6. spread and sprinkle over each
7. serve

shrimp à la Marx canapé

ingredients:

(see page 60)

procedure:

1. drain

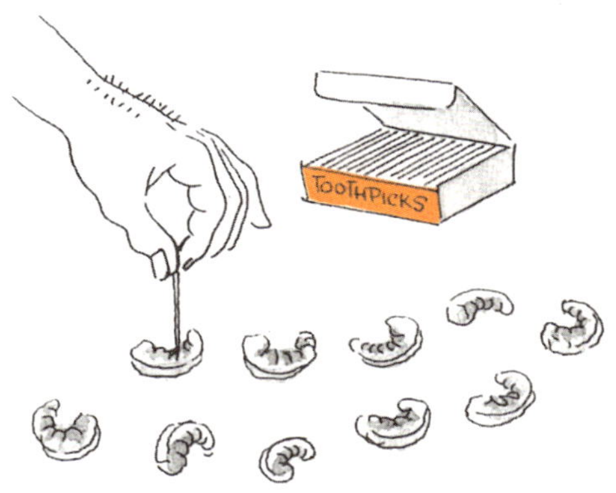

2. impale each

3. pour into glass bowl

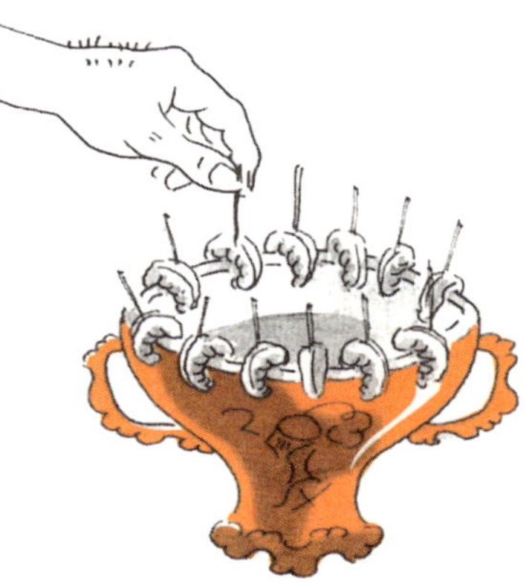

4. arrange so

canapé olive chaud

ingredients:

procedure:

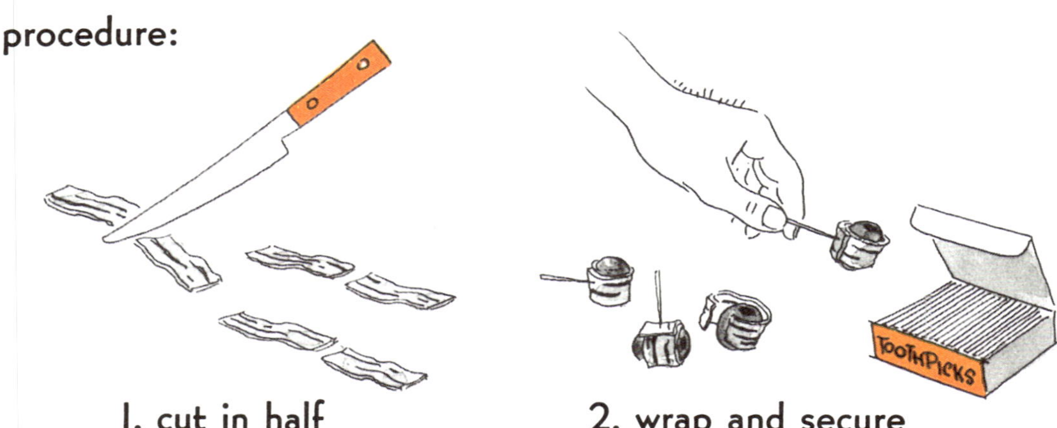

1. cut in half

2. wrap and secure

3. broil

4. remove and serve pronto

PART VII

drinks

the host's liquid assets

YOU can lead a guest to water but you can't make him drink — not if it's firewater he wants. And — a guest can lead his host to the bar but can't make him mix a drink either — not if he doesn't know how.

How do we know? Surveys, of course! There's been the Gallup Poll and the Roper Poll and the Kinsey Report, and now there's the BINGEY REPORT, conducted solely to compile the data for our subject matter, liquid hosting. In the process of this survey we uncovered some of the most amazing facts about the drinking habits germane to the American male:

1. He will experiment with utter abandon with a variety of drink methods — when at a bar.
2. He will even encourage his companion to experiment with the drink fantastic, and is as adventuresome as any red-blooded pioneer of old —when at a bar.
3. When this identical bold adventurer is at home and is confronted with mixing anything other than a whiskey straight (or with soda), he's as a timid as a bride (of old).
4. 96.8% OF AMERICAN MALES ARE DRINK-TENDER VIRGINS.

The purpose, therefore, of this entire section is to introduce the adult male to the true facts of fermentation so it can be enjoyed with the maximum of tempered pleasure.

After a very profound (but delightful) study, verified by the terrifying conclusions of the BINGEY survey, here is the basic law of liquids which, in its way, is just as vital as Boyle's Law concerning gaseous matter:

LAW OF LIQUID REFRESHMENT (especially those fermented): *Omnes drinks divisae sunt in partes quinque!* Using a standard "pony," this is translated as, "All drinks are divided into five parts":

1. Cocktail-hour drinks
2. Before-dinner drinks
3. Drinks with meals
4. After-dinner drinks
5. Drinks that have nothing to do with meals (for card parties, social gatherings, and general conviviality)

For further details, read on —

this is what you need in way of basic fuel

basic implements
cocktail shaker
squeezer
spoon and opener
corkscrew
ice strainer
jigger
muddler
ice-cube bowl
basic containers
cocktail
Collins
Highball
Old Fashioned
Drink
Cognac
Liqueur
coasters
Sherry
Here are all the measuring symbols you have to know:
jigger (1¾ oz.)
½ half-jigger
teaspoon
half-teaspoon
a dash of
Note all recipes are for one drink only - multiply where necessary

PART VIII

dissolving the five o'clock shadow

or the cocktail hour

PEOPLE are strange. When you invite them for cocktails, they expect cocktails — they are unreasonable that way. But what's even more strange, there's many a host who makes this grandiose invitation: "Drop over for a cocktail around five." And what happens? The guest arrives, parched and expectant, and is offered his choice of whiskey and water or soda. That's the host's entire repertoire.

The moral of this story is: when you do invite guests for cocktails, remember — they expect cocktails. And — all you have to do to be able to shake — or stir — a potent potable is to read on and follow the pictures.

horse's neck really
ingredients:
GIN
GINGER ALE
SUGAR
GIN
SUGAR
GINGER ALE
1. peel and drape
2. add
3. add–fill–serve
whiskey sour
ingredients:
RYE
SODA
SUGAR
Maraschino CHERRIES
RYE
SODA
SUGAR
Maraschino CHERRIES
1. squeeze–add
2. add and shake
3. pour–garnish–serve

orange blossom

ingredients:

1. mix

2. add and shake

3. pour—garnish

daiquiri

ingredients:

1. mix

2. add
shake till frosted

3. pour—serve

sidecar

ingredients:

piscolabis

ingredients:

1. crack and fill

2. add

3. stir—garnish—serve

bluebell

ingredients:

1. mix

2. add

3. shake—serve

comin' thro' the rye

ingredients:

1. mix

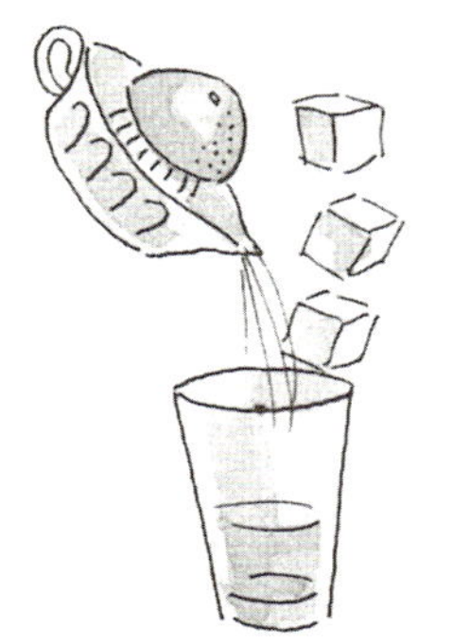

2. add

3. pour—serve

rob roy

ingredients:

1. mix

2. ice–stir

3. garnish–serve

rum and maple

ingredients:

1. mix

2. add

3. shake–serve

PART IX

before-dinner drinks

aperitifs and cocktails

WHY drinks before meals?

Whether you're host to one or one hundred, no matter the sex involved, each must be wooed like a woman, gently, subtly, and with perfect timing and priming. For a guest, newly arrived at your home, is a xenophobic animal, on edge with suspicions and fears: his host may have Borgia tendencies at mealtime. The other guests may be an insidious mixture of pickpockets, undercover agents, rakes, and/or adventuresses — or worse still — all bores.

But ply this quivering creature with just the right kind of drink and he becomes calm, conversational, convivial, and most receptive to both your guests and to your efforts as a host. So here are the requisites for wooing your dinner guest, as you prime his salivaries.

bacardi cocktail

ingredients:

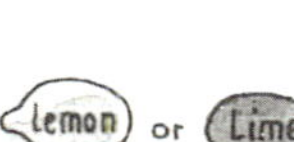

1. mix

2. shake

3. serve

bamboo cocktail

ingredients:

1. mix

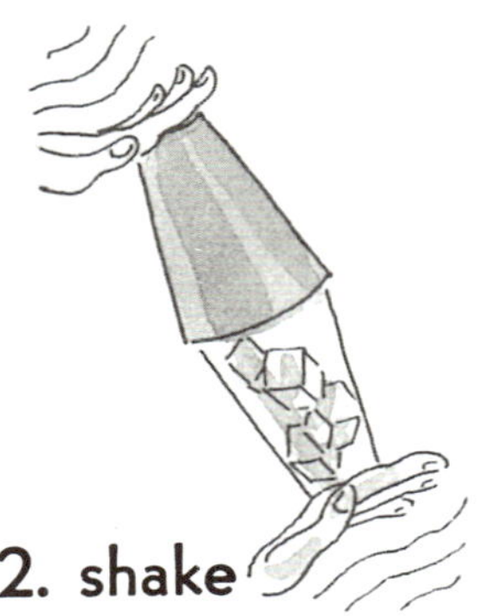

2. shake

3. serve

brandy cocktail

Bronx cocktail

ingredients:

Delmonico cocktail

ingredients:

1. mix

2. ice—stir

3. pour

Manhattan cocktail

ingredients:

1. mix

2. ice—stir

3. pour and add

Martini cocktail

ingredients:

1. mix

2. ice—stir very thoroughly

3. pour—add

subversive Martini cocktail

ingredients:

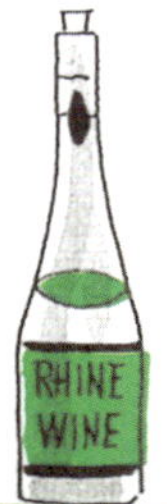

1. mix

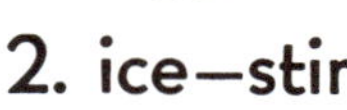

2. ice—stir

3. pour and twist

Martini esoterica
cocktail

ingredients: 

1. mix

2. ice—stir *well*

3. pour and add

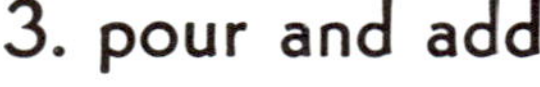

old fashioned
cocktail

ingredients: 

1. muddle

2. add and muddle

3. add—
stir—garnish

PART X

drinks with meals

or how to float a dessert

"A jug of wine, a loaf of bread — and thou beside me singing in the wilderness."

A delightful situation.

But if thou, bud, doth not have the correct wine with the loaf, thou wilt be singing in the wilderness — alone!

Did you know, for example, that white wine with steak is a faux pas; that red wine with chicken may be a subversive gaucherie; that beer with dessert is a capital crime?

The correct drinks to serve with meals is a very ticklish subject. Your entire social future can be destroyed by not knowing what to serve with what. So to spare you such an anchorite, antisocial dilemma, here is a chart to guide you through the unchartered Sahara of an eight-course meal — right through dessert.

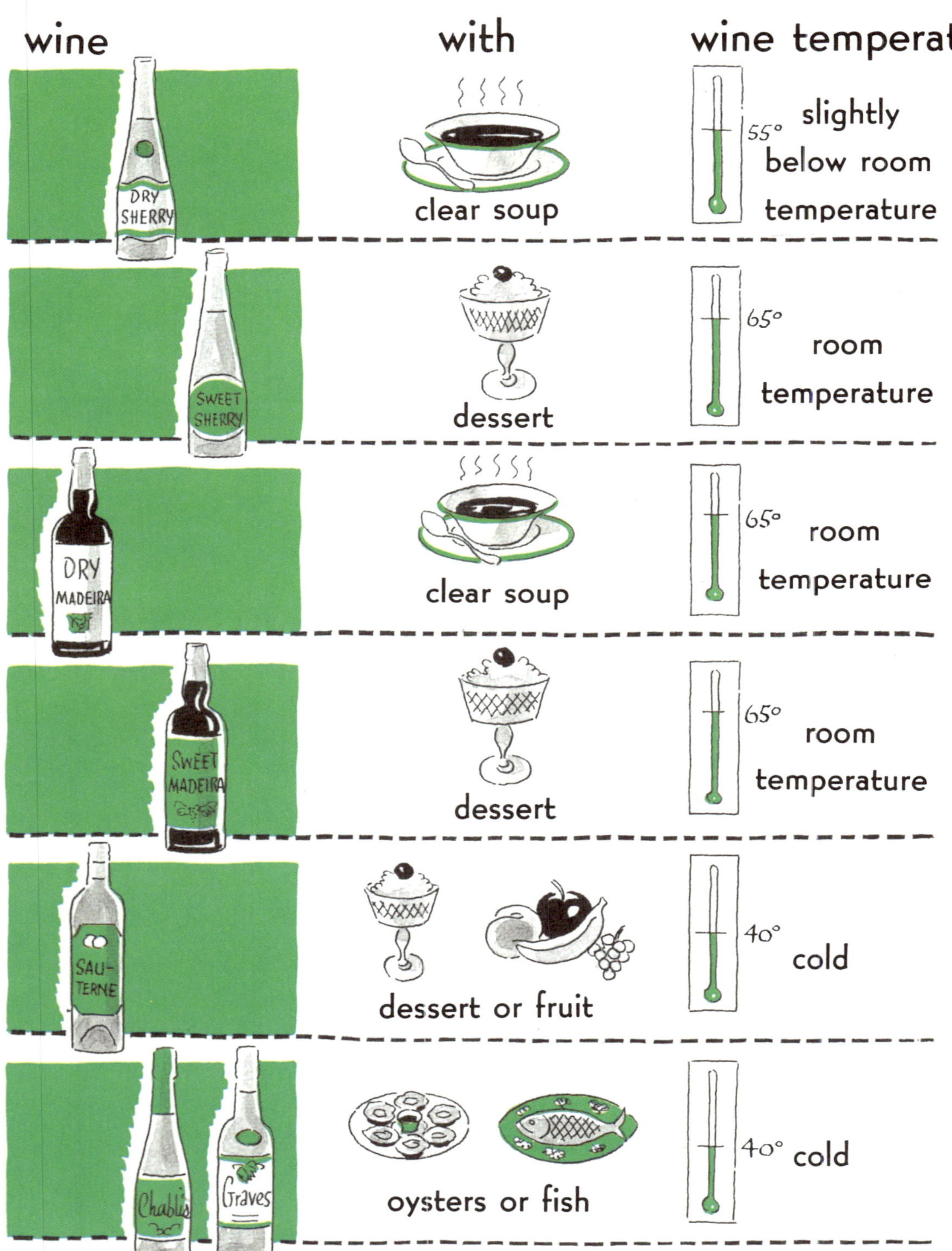
wine
with
wine temperature
DRY SHERRY
clear soup
55°
slightly below room temperature
SWEET SHERRY
dessert
65°
room temperature
DRY MADEIRA
clear soup
65°
room temperature
SWEET MADEIRA
dessert
65°
room temperature
SAU-TERNE
dessert or fruit
40°
cold
Chablis
Graves
oysters or fish
40°
cold

wine
with
wine temperature
RHINE
Moselle
fish
45°
below room temperature
RED Burgundy
steak or venison
65°
room temperature
CLARET
CHIANTI
roast, chicken, or salad
65°
room temperature
DRY Champagne
fish (also entire meal)
32°
PORT
cheese
65°
room temperature
Malaga
Muscatel
dessert
65°
room temperature

PART XI

after-dinner drinks

A well-fed after-dinner guest is a fatted calf — ready for the slow torture of postprandial discomfort. His eyes are glazed, his mind is dazed — he's an inert mass of gastrointestinal activity.

But there's a cure. It's continental, elemental, and an extremely cordial form of resuscitation — with liqueur.

There are more cordials on the market than there are nationalities. On the following pages, however, are depicted only those which have the international stamp of approval. And no esoteric legerdemain is required to serve them other than an ample supply — and some liqueur glasses. Only in a few instances is any form of mixing a requisite.

So to resurrect your sluggish guest — pour on.

your liqueur store

the liqueur glass
for all cordials shown
except cognac

the brandy glass
for cognac
snifting

b and b
ingredients:
BENEDICTINE
BRANDY
BRANDY
BENEDICTINE
2. complete
1. fill half way
c and c
ingredients:
coffee
lump sugar
COGNAC
procedure:
demitasse cup
1. pour
COGNAC
2. place and fill
3. ignite and let burn
4. pour

PART XII

drinks that have nothing to do with meals

THIS is the last chapter, the last verse, on drink etiquette.

Liquors were not merely brewed and fermented to abet one's gustatory powers. A drink, partaken of with proper discretion, acts as a pleasant thirst-quencher, a chill-destroyer, and a social-cementer. Served at card parties, dances, or even gatherings of intellectual pundits, it releases tensions and dissolves unnecessary taboos.

In fact, an alcoholic beverage is a social cyclotron breaking down the self-contained atoms (your guests) and dispersing the neutrons, deuterons, electrons, and persons equitably so that a pleasant mixture of personalities results.

So when a crowd descends upon you for an evening of bridge or poker, or just for conviviality at your expense, do you know what to serve? Or on a long, hot summer's afteroon, what to quaff? Or on a bleak, black winter's day, what to snift?

Read on.

Bourbon highball (cold weather)

ingredients:

1. pour

2. add

brandy highball (cold weather)

ingredients:

1. pour

2. add

champagne punch (hot or cold weather—you won't know the difference)

eggnog

for eggmas cheer (cold weather)

ingredients:

serves 8 or more

procedure:

1. separate and beat each

2. add and beat in

3. and beat in

4. stir in gently and sprinkle

Cuban cola (hot weather)

ingredients:

procedure:

1. squeeze — add

2. add — stir — serve

French "75"

(hot weather)

ingredients:

procedure:

1. squeeze

2. add

3. fill — stir — quaff

mint julep (hot weather)
CCQ
ingredients:
mint
Bourbon
SUGAR
shaved ice
procedure:
HOT
SUGAR
1. crush
2. add and crush
3. add and crush
shaved ice
Bourbon
4. pack solid—add
5. juggle—stir
until frost forms on
outside of glass
6. garnish—sip

brandy smash
ingredients:
mint
strawberries
orange slice
BRANDY
SUGAR
shaved ice
SUGAR
BRANDY
shaved ice
2/3
1. put in
2. add and pack
3. garnish—sip
HOT WEATHER
planter's punch
ingredients:
orange slice
lime
JAMAICA RUM
Maraschino CHERRIES
SUGAR
SUGAR
JAMAICA RUM
1. put in—squeeze
2. add
3. garnish—guzzle

rum Collins
ingredients:
Cuban RUM
SODA
SUGAR
SUGAR
Cuban RUM
SODA
1. put in and squeeze
2. add
3. add—serve
HOT WEATHER
Tom Collins
ingredients:
GIN
SODA
SUGAR
SUGAR
GIN
SODA
1. put in and squeeze
2. add
3. add—serve

Scotch and soda

(hot or cold weather)

ingredients:

1. put in

2. add and serve

rye highball

(hot or cold weather)

ingredients:

1. put in

2. add and serve

the screwdriver
ingredients:
VODKA
ORANGE JUICE
VODKA
ORANGE JUICE
1. pour over ice cubes
2. fill with orange juice—stir well

index

drinks

this space for

favorite dishes

this space for

favorite dishes